Pearson

Year 2

Handwriting
Activity Workbook

Home learning from the experts

Author:

Sarah Loader

About this book

This book supports the practice and consolidation of handwriting skills, with lots of engaging, fun activities to help children grow in confidence and ability.

Clear, consistent, cursive handwriting is not only a statutory requirement of the English curriculum, but is the gateway to success in all subjects. The ability to present ideas legibly and coherently is a critical life skill.

Handwriting made clear

- Handwriting requires strong fine-motor skills and pencil control, which can be challenging for children of all ages. The tasks in this activity book develop and finesse those skills.
- Key skills are learned and reinforced through a wide range of tasks to keep children engaged and interested in each activity.
- Helpful tips and reminders support children as they work.
- Progression is ensured through the careful development of clarity and consistency in handwriting presentation.

How to use this book

- Little-and-often is a productive approach to handwriting, as handwriting requires great concentration and can be frustrating. Children can work through just one or two activities in a sitting, and stop when they lose interest to avoid it becoming negative.
- Try to complete the activities in the given order, as they progress in challenge and expectation.
- Your child will ideally work through activities independently, but it's worth being there for when support is needed.
- Explore the Progress Points with your child as they work through the book to see where further support is needed.

Getting started

- Make your child's learning space interesting and fun, in a favourite place to sit or with a favourite toy beside them.
- Encourage your child to step away from any technology or energetic games a little while beforehand, and to take some deep breaths to help them focus.
- Make sure your child is holding their pencil properly.
- Sit with your child to start, even if you're occupied with your own task.

Challenges to overcome

Forming letters in proportion to each other

Due to the sustained control required, and because children initially learn to create one letter at a time, it is tricky for them to keep the letters of whole words and sentences the right size in relation to each other – particularly with capital and lower-case letters. Learning how to write these side by side is practised throughout this book.

Using spaces between words

As children begin to write whole sentences they need to measure out spaces between each word. Using their finger to do this is good practice and avoids words running into each other, which is a common trait of early writing.

Starting to join letters

In Year 2 children start to use cursive, or joined-up writing. It's important for children to get plenty of practice with how joins are formed, so this feature becomes an increased focus as children work their way through this book.

Get creative

- Postal addresses are a good format for practising writing capital and lower-case letters side by side as they appear a lot in a small amount of text. You could ask children to copy out addresses from post that arrives or from your address book.
- Creating name cards for family and/or friends is another way to practise writing capital and lower-case letters in proportion.
- Some children may still need to develop their understanding of the different letter families, so creating a collage of letters for each family from newspapers and magazines is good practice.
- Because cursive writing relies on more relaxed, flowing shapes, finding patterns and mazes to trace is a useful strategy to hone this skill.

English curriculum coverage

As well as covering the Year 2 handwriting statutory requirements, this activity book develops and practises handwriting skills within the context of the wider English curriculum, so that tasks and activities are meaningful and relevant for children. For extended practice, the following topics are also covered. Note that some of these are taken from the previous year's objectives as a useful form of revision and reinforcement.

Topic	Curriculum relevance
suffixes –ing, –est, –er and –ed	Writing – Transcription (Year 1 programme of study)
suffixes –ment, –ness, –less, –ful and –ly	Writing – Transcription (Year 2 programme of study)
Homophones	English Appendix 1: Spelling (work for Year 2)
Spelling the days of the week	Writing – Transcription (Year 1 programme of study)

Activity 1

Trace and write these capital and lower-case letters.

Start each stroke at a red dot.

Aa

Bb

Cc

Dd

Ee

Ff

Activity 2

Rewrite the name and address using the correct capital letters.

abigail clark
2 drummers avenue
borchester
england

Abigail

Activity 3

> The letters in these words are mixed up.
> Write them out correctly.

i b d r _____

g o f r _____

y l j e l _____

i p s h _____

Activity 4

> The words in these sentences are mixed up.
> Write them out correctly.

small. is hat too My

_____

queen happy. The very is

_____

of lots fish. are There

_____

Activity 5

Trace and write these capital and lower-case letters.

Gg

Hh

Ii

Jj

Kk

Ll

Mm

Activity 6

Write your full name and address on this envelope. Remember to use capital letters

Activity 7

Write a word in each gap to complete these sentences.

_____ Aunt Kate,

___ hope you _____ well. ___ am having a _____

holiday. It is _____ and sunny. I _____

to the beach and _____ with my friends.

From _____

Activity 8

Trace and write these capital and lower-case letters.

Nn   Nn Nn

Oo   Oo Oo

Pp   Pp Pp

Qq   Qq Qq

Rr   Rr Rr

Ss   Ss Ss

Tt   Tt Tt

Activity 9

> The letters in these words are mixed up.
> Write them out correctly.

ishf  _____

eenqu  _____

toab  _____

napad _____

Activity 10

> The words in these sentences are mixed up.
> Write them out correctly.

bird see a can I.

_____

_____

an ago. boat The hour left

_____

_____

Sunday. rains on It always

_____

_____

Activity 11

Trace and write these capital and lower-case letters.

Uu Uu Uu

Vv Vv Vv

Ww Ww Ww

Xx Xx Xx

Yy Yy Yy

Zz Zz Zz

I | I can write my letters at the right size.

Activity 12

The sentences in this postcard are mixed up. Write them out correctly, adding capital letters in the correct places.

i cannot wait! i miss you. it is very cold here. dear mum and dad, i hope i don't fall. today we are going sledging. love from hasan

Dear

Activity 13

Write your own postcard home. You can use the words in the box to help you. Remember to use full stops and capital letters.

dear cold hot sunny snow

beach mountains swim sledge

skate fish go very miss home

Dear

Activity 14

Underline all the tall letters and circle all the descender letters.

s a t p i n m d g o c k

Activity 15

Write six words using the letters in the box above.

Make your tall letters reach up and your descender letters drop down.

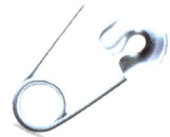

Activity 16

> Rewrite these sentences using the correct capital letters.

we do art on mondays.

We do

on tuesdays we have football.

we have pasta on a wednesday.

our school trip is on thursday.

this friday, connor is coming.

i play with rex on saturday.

we go swimming on sundays

Activity 17

Underline all the tall letters and circle all the descender letters.

s   a   t   p   i   n   m   d   g

o   c   k   e   u   r   h   b   f

Activity 18

Write six words using the letters in the box above.

_____

_____

_____

_____

_____

_____

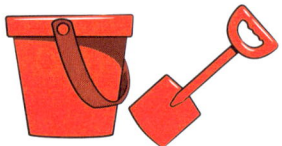

2 I know the tall- and descender-letter families.

Activity 19

Draw lines to match each word to the correct ending. Then write out the words in full.

These endings are called suffixes.

build

high

sprint

cold

jump

fast

small

play

watch

low

ing

est

building

Activity 20

These root words and suffixes are the wrong way around. Write them out correctly.

ingjump

estsmall

estfast

ingplay

Activity 21

The words in these sentences are mixed up. Write them out correctly.

event The sprinting brilliant. was

a tower. building is Lee

3 I can write words with suffixes –ing and –est.

Activity 22

Draw lines to match each word to the correct ending. Then write out the words in full.

Remember where the small, tall and descender letters sit.

quick

smart

strong

pull

dark

ask

quiet

open

fresh

wait

er

ed

quicker

Activity 23

Use the words in the box to complete the sentences.

asked smarter pulled longer
darker lighter

1. Abby is _____ than you think.

2. There was a creak as I _____ the gate open.

3. It got _____ as the sun rose.

4. Kam _____ for an extra bun.

5. It is much _____ without the night-light.

6. Mark has _____ hair than Asif.

Activity 24

The words in these sentences are mixed up. Write them out correctly.

Start each sentence with a capital letter and use finger spaces between words.

1. opened he door. the

He opened the door.

2. stronger is Adnan Martin. than

3. the waited she gate. school Mum for at

4. it country. the quieter in is

5. asked extra for Kit homework.

6. smarter is Symona me. than

4 I can write words with suffixes –er and –ed.

Activity 25

Draw lines to match each word to the correct ending.
Then write out the words in full.

improve

enjoy

sad

kind

ment

excite

sweet

ness

disappoint

fit

achieve

fair

Activity 26

The mistakes in this text have been circled. Write out the text correctly.

My teacher said that in (fairment) there was some (improvment) in my writing, but that there was still not enough (excitness). If I want to see real (achievment), I need to work harder.

_____

_____

_____

----

5 I can write words with suffixes –ment and –ness.

Activity 27

> Draw lines to match each word to the correct ending.
> Then write out the words in full.

| play |

| care |

| delight |

| home | | less |

| sad |

| slow | | ful |

| respect |

| need |

| quick | | ly |

| truth |

Activity 28

Write out these sentences, choosing a root word and the correct suffix to complete each one.

Root words	**Suffixes**
home delight play truth careful	–less –ful –ly

1. Our new kitten is very _____?_____.

2. What a _____?_____ house.

3. It is so _____?_____ by the fire.

4. Cross the road _____?_____.

5. Always be _____?_____.

6 I can write words with suffixes –less, –ful, –ly.

Activity 29

Write out the sentences, choosing the correct homophone to complete each one.

Homophones are words that sound the same, but have different spellings and meanings.

1. The (sea / see) was bright blue.

_____

_____

_____

2. The (bare / bear) lay in the woods.

_____

_____

_____

3. Lunch is at (one / won) o'clock.

_____

_____

_____

4. It was a dark (night / knight).

_____

_____

_____

5. His (sun / son) works at the bakery.

_____

_____

_____

Activity 30

The wrong homophones have been used in this text.
Circle the mistakes and then write out the text correctly.
Remember to use capital letters and finger spaces.

It was a dark, windy knight. The son had gone down and I was alone. There was no won around, not a single person. As it got darker, I could sea less and less.

Activity 31

Trace and write the joined-up letters.

ul ul

th th

al al

mu mu

Activity 32

Trace the patterns.

Activity 33

Trace and write the joined-up letters.

it   it

my   my

at   at

in   in

Activity 34

Trace and write out the words with joined-up letters for the pairs.

bat   bit

win   pat

8 I can join two letters together.

Activity 35

Trace and write out the words with joined-up letters.

hit   hit

hat   hat

all   all

the   the

mum   mum

cat   cat

nit   nit

nap   nap

Activity 36

Trace and write out the sentences.

Keep practising those joined-up letters!

I hit the ball with my bat.

The ball hit the hut.

The hut fell flat.

9 I can join three letters together.

My name is